Collins

Easy Learning

Comprehension practice

Age 7-9

My name is _____Sam_____.

I am _____9_____ years old.

I go to _____ School.

My birthday is _____.

How to use this book

- Find a quiet, comfortable place to work, away from other distractions.
- Tackle one extract at a time.
- It is important that your child reads the extract and questions carefully.
- Help with reading the extract and instructions where necessary, and ensure your child understands what to do.

- Encourage your child to check their own answers as they complete each activity.
- Discuss your child's answers with them.
- Let your child return to their favourite pages once they have been completed. Talk about the extracts.
- Reward your child with plenty of praise and encouragement.

Comprehension

Comprehension exercises teach children important skills.

Comprehension questions cover three main categories:

1 *Literal questions* are where the child is required to find and summarise information from the extract.

2 *Inferential questions* are where the child is required to make deductions and predictions from the information provided in the extract.

3 *Evaluative questions* are where the child is required to criticise, empathise with, and relate their own experiences to questions.

This book includes a mixture of these question types, so that your child becomes familiar with each one.

This book also includes a variety of different types of comprehension so that your child can practise understanding and answering questions on different types of comprehension (see table alongside).

Published by Collins
An imprint of HarperCollins*Publishers*
77–85 Fulham Palace Road
Hammersmith
London
W6 8JB

Browse the complete Collins catalogue at
www.collins.co.uk

© HarperCollins*Publishers* 2011

10 9 8 7 6 5 4 3 2

ISBN-13 978-0-00-746159-2

Acknowledgements
Every effort has been made to trace copyright holders and to obtain their permission for the use of copyright material. The author and publishers will gladly receive any information enabling them to rectify any error or omission in subsequent editions.

The publisher wishes to thank the following for permission to use copyright materials:

David Higham Associates Limited for the poem *I Love Our Orange Tent* from *Story Chest: Poet's Corner – Big Bulgy Fat Black Slugs* by Berlie Doherty, Nelson Thornes Ltd, copyright ©Berlie Doherty; United Agents for an extract from *In the Rue Bel Tesoro* by Lin Coghlan ©Lin Coghlan; *Thunder and Lightning, Motorway madness, Basilisks, Oceans Alive, An Ants' Nest, On the move, Adventure park* copyright ©John Jackman; Poem *A Small Dragon* from *Collected Love Poems* by Brian Patten. Reprinted by permission of HarperCollins*Publishers* Ltd © 2007 Brian Patten; HarperCollins*Publishers* Inc for an extract from "The Golly Sisters Go West" by Betsy Byars, copyright ©1985 Betsy Byars.

Illustration on p.29 © David Fairfield / Thinkstock.com

British Library Cataloguing in Publication Data

A Catalogue record for this publication is available from the British Library

Page layout by Linda Miles, Lodestone Publishing Ltd
Illustrated by Kathy Baxendale
Cover design by Linda Miles, Lodestone Publishing Ltd
Cover illustration by Kathy Baxendale
Project managed by Katie Galloway
Printed and bound in China
Commissioned by Tammy Poggo

MIX
Paper from
responsible sources
FSC® C007454

FSC™ is a non-profit international organisation established to promote the responsible management of the world's forests. Products carrying the FSC label are independently certified to assure consumers that they come from forests that are managed to meet the social, economic and ecological needs of present and future generations, and other controlled sources.

Find out more about HarperCollins and the environment at
www.harpercollins.co.uk/green

Contents

The Golly Sisters sat in their wagon. They were going west.
"Go," May-May said to the horse.
The horse did not go.

"This makes me mad," May-May said.
"Our wagon is ready. Our songs and dances are ready.
And the horse will not go."

"It makes me mad too," said Rose.
"Something is wrong with this horse."

Rose got down from the wagon. May-May got down too.
They walked around the horse.

"Do you see something wrong?" May-May asked.
"No, but something is wrong," said Rose.
"When we say, 'Go', the horse does not go."
"And if the horse does not go, we do not go," said May-May.

Suddenly, Rose said, "Sister! I just remembered something.
There is a horse word for 'go'."
"A horse word?" said May-May.
"What is it?"
"Giddy-up!" Rose said.

The horse went.

From The Golly Sisters Go West *by Betsy Byars*

Complete the sentences.

Q1 May-May and Rose are the _____ Sisters.

Q2 The sisters were going _____.

Q3 _____ got down from the wagon first.

Q4 The sisters looked at the _____ to see if anything was wrong.

Q5 _____ _____ wrote this story.

Answer each of the questions with a sentence.

Q6 Why did the sisters want to go west?

_____

Q7 Did the sisters find anything wrong with the horse?

_____

Q8 Why did the horse not move when the sisters said 'Go'?

_____

Q9 What did the sisters say to make the horse move?

_____

Q10 How do you think the sisters felt before and after the horse moved? Write five words in each box to describe their feelings.

Before	After

I love our orange tent.
We plant it <u>like</u> a flower in the field.   *feel*
The grass smells sweet inside it.

And at night
When we're lying in it,
I hear the owl crying.

When the wind blows,
my tent flaps
like a flying bird.

And the rain
patters down on it
with tiny footsteps.

I feel warm and safe
inside my tent.

But when the sun shines,
that's when I love it best!

When I wake up
and the sun is shining,
it pours in like yellow honey.
It glows like gold.

I love our orange tent.

Berlie Doherty

Tick (✔) the true statements and cross (✗) the false statements.

Q1 The tent is orange. ☐

Q2 Inside the tent there is the sweet smell of grass. ☐

Q3 The tent is likened to a shed in a field. ☐

Q4 The rain makes the tent flap like a flying bird. ☐

Q5 The poet likes to be in the tent when the sun shines. ☐

Q6 When the sun shines the tent smells like yellow honey. ☐

Answer each of the questions with a sentence.

Q7 Which line in the poem is repeated?

_____

Q8 Why do you think the poet repeats this line?

_____

Q9 Which verse describes the poet feeling safe in the orange tent?

_____

Q10 Do you think the poet would still describe the tent as glowing 'like gold' if it was a blue tent? Why?

_____

Q11 How would you feel if you were camping in a tent and there was loud thunder and lightning in the middle of the night? Describe what you see, hear and feel.

_____

_____

Thunder and Lightning

Thunder and Lightning were two grumpy old sheep.

Lightning would lose his temper and knock down trees and burn the crops. Thunder, his mother who had an extremely loud voice, would shout at him.

The villagers became really fed up with them. The villagers kept complaining about the damage – and the noise!

In the end, the village chief said he couldn't stand it any longer. He said they would have to go far away. He sent them to live in the sky!

But things didn't work out as the chief intended. To this day, Lightning still enjoys getting his own back on the villagers, and Thunder still shouts at the top of her voice and keeps the villagers awake at night.

Nigerian folk story

Complete these sentences.

Q1 Thunder and Lightning are two _grumpy old sheep_ .

Q2 Thunder would shout at _lightning_ .

Q3 The villagers complained about the _damige_ and _the noise_

Q4 The village chief sent Thunder and Lightning to the _sky_ .

Q5 _thunder_ still keeps the villagers awake at night.

Q6 'Thunder and Lightning' is a _Nigerian_ folk story.

Q7 Write words to describe how the villagers first felt when the sheep were sent to the sky and then after they had been there for a while.

Villagers' feelings at first	Villagers' feelings after a while
rdeafed	anoid

Answer each of the questions with a sentence.

Q8 Why do you think the village chief decided to banish Thunder and Lightning to the sky?

I think the chielB was angrey at all the distruchen they were making so he banished them.

Q9 How do you think Thunder and Lightning felt when they were sent to the sky?

I think thunder and lightni were furios whent they were sent away.

Cheeky chimps on the motorway

Drivers were surprised to see monkeys running all over the road yesterday.

The lorry taking them to their new home at Burwell Zoo had broken down. While the driver went to get help, one of the monkeys managed to lift the latch on the door.

Inspector Baker said the monkeys looked like they were having great fun.

They climbed all over the road signs and scrambled up the lamp posts. One even sat on top of the police car!

Some drivers got irate because of the traffic jam, but most drivers were prepared to see the funny side.

"I'm pleased to say all the cheeky chimps are now safely back in the zoo," said Inspector Baker last night.

Q1 Copy these sentences, putting them in the correct order.

A monkey sat on top of a police car.
A lorry carrying monkeys broke down.
The monkeys safely arrived at the zoo.
The lorry driver went to get help.
A monkey lifted the latch on the lorry door.

1. _____

2. _____

3. _____

4. _____

5. _____

Answer each of the questions with a sentence.

Q2 How do you think the lorry driver felt?

_____

Q3 How do you think Inspector Baker felt?

_____

Q4 Imagine you were in a car watching the monkeys. Write a short recount, describing what you saw and how it made you feel.

_____

_____

_____

_____

_____

One day a mouse happened to run over the paws of a sleeping lion. Angrily the mighty beast woke. He was about to crush the little animal when the mouse cried out, "Please, mighty king of all animals, spare me. I would be only a tiny mouthful, and I'm sure you would not like the taste. Besides, I might be able to help you some day. You never can tell."

The idea that the tiny creature could ever help him amused the lion so much that he let his little prisoner go.

Some time after this the lion, roaming in the forest for food, was caught in a hunter's net. The more he struggled the more he became stuck; his roar of rage echoed through the forest. Hearing the sound the mouse ran to the trap and began to gnaw the ropes that bound the lion. It was not long before he had bitten through the last cord with his little teeth and set the huge beast free. and

trast a lion

Don't belittle little things.

Aesop's Fables

lion atehim

Answer each of the questions with a sentence.

walk

Q1 How did the mouse wake the lion?

by walking on its paws.

Q2 Why did the lion let the mouse go?

said

because the mouse ~~said~~ he would
help him one day.

Q3 What did the lion become caught in?

maybe

hmmmmm ... maby a net

Q4 How did the lion escape?

because of the mouse

Q5 Find a word in the extract that means the same
as these words.

small   little

flatten   crushed

wandering   roming

nibble   gnaw

large   huge

Q6 There is a moral to this story: **Don't belittle little things.**
What do you think this moral means? (Look up the meaning of 'belittle'.)

fun of

don't tease or make a little
little people

Faster than fairies, faster than witches,
Bridges and houses, hedges and ditches;
And charging along like troops in a battle,
All through the meadows the horses and cattle;
All of the sights of the hill and the plain
Fly as thick as driving rain;
And ever again, in the wink of an eye,
Painted stations whistle by.

Here is a child who clambers and scrambles,
All by himself and gathering brambles;
Here is a tramp who stands and gazes;
And there is the green for stringing the daisies!
Here is a cart run away in the road
Lumping along with man and load;
And here is a mill, and there is a river:
Each a glimpse and gone for ever!

R. L. Stevenson

Complete the sentences using the correct options.

Q1 The poem is written from a _____.

       moving car   **railway bank**   **moving railway carriage**

Q2 The railway carriage passes _____.

    fairies and witches   **bridges and houses**   **a man walking a dog**

Q3 A _____ watches the railway carriage go by.

               tramp   **woman**   **child**

Q4 The cart is carrying _____.

    troops to a battle   **a pile of brambles**   **a man and load**

Answer the questions.

Q5 Write the word in the poem that rhymes with:

    cattle _____   plain _____   brambles _____

Q6 How do we know this poem was written a long time ago?

_____

Q7 What does the poet mean by 'Each a glimpse and gone for ever!'?

_____

Q8 Think of a short journey you have made in a car.
Using sentences, describe four things you remember passing.

    I. _____

    2. _____

    3. _____

    4. _____

Oceans Alive

Contents

Written by Angie Belcher
Photographed by Andy Belcher

Collins

Complete these sentences.

Q1 The title of the book is _Oceans Alive_.

Q2 The book is written by _Angie Belcher_.

Q3 _Collins_ are the publishers of the book.

Q4 The glossary can be found on page _44_.

Q5 The chapter about _Oeans under threat_ can be found on page 22.

Write a number to answer each of these questions.

Q6 How many chapters are there? _8 11_

Q7 On which page would you start reading about new discoveries? _38_

Q8 On which page can you read about saving the oceans? _22_

Q9 On which page would you start reading about life in the ocean? _9_

Q10 On which page might you find the meaning of a word? _44_

Q11 How many pages are there in the longest chapter? _10 16_

Answer each question in sentences.

Q12 If you were asked to add a chapter to this book what would it be about? What title would you give it?

I would call it Predators and Prey

Q13 A book blurb is the short description on the back of a book that tells you what the book is about. Write a short book blurb for this book.

This book is about the oceans and how we can save it.

Basilisks

Once upon a time, in a far off land, a strange thing happened, a very strange thing indeed. A snake laid an egg, which is not unusual for a reptile. Then, through the grass came a cockerel. The cockerel sat upon the egg and kept it warm, and sure enough, after a time the shell began to crack. At this the cockerel stalked away through the tall, dark grass.

From the broken shell emerged a strange and scary creature. It had the feet, body, wings and head of a cockerel, but the tail twisted and turned and it had the long, forked darting tongue of a snake. The eyes were the protruding eyes of a toad.

This was the myth of the basilisk, said to be a very harmful monster. Any plant it touched would dry up and die; any rock it touched would break. Even its breath could kill a person. In fact, just a look from the beast could kill. A man on horseback could stab a basilisk, but then the poison would climb the spear and the man would die, and so would his horse. There was said to be only one way to kill a basilisk – with a mirror. If the basilisk looked in the mirror its own glance would kill it.

People believed in basilisks for hundreds of years. In 1587 in Warsaw, Poland, two small girls were found dead in a cellar. Rumours circulated that a basilisk was to blame. Someone had an idea. There was a criminal about to be put to death for his crimes, so what did it matter if a basilisk killed him?

The criminal put on a leather suit, covered in mirrors, and went down into the cellar. When he emerged he was carrying something. At first it looked like a dead snake, but could it be a dead basilisk? Who knew? Few people had ever seen a real one, and those who had seen one had died. At last the king's doctor was called in. He studied the beast.

"Yes," he said, "definitely a basilisk."

Use words from the box to finish each sentence.

> mirror   basilisk   doctor   egg   Poland   cockerel

Q1 An _____ was laid by a snake.

Q2 The _____ kept it warm.

Q3 The animal that appeared was known as a _____.

Q4 The only way to kill the monster was with a _____.

Q5 Two girls were found dead in a cellar in _____.

Q6 People asked the king's _____ what had killed the girls.

Q7 Using the picture and information from the passage, write a detailed description of the basilisk.

_____

_____

_____

Answer each of the questions with a sentence.

Q8 If you were the criminal who went into the cellar, how do you think you would have felt?

_____

Q9 Why do you think the king's doctor was called to study the beast?

_____

Q10 How do you think people in Warsaw felt when it was confirmed that the girls were killed by a basilisk?

_____

Inside the nest

Tiny tunnels lead into the nest.
Each nest is a mass of tunnels and rooms.

Types of ants

In every nest there are three types of ant.
The biggest are the queen ants. Queen ants have wings.
The big males also have wings, but aren't quite as big.
The small ants are the worker ants, and they don't have wings.

Who does what?

A queen ant lives in one room of the nest. She stays in her room all the time
and lays hundreds of eggs.

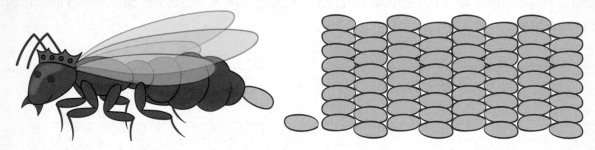

The big male ants mate with a queen, then die.

The worker ants collect the food. They feed the young ants, keep the nest clean,
and dig more rooms and tunnels as they are needed. They also keep away ants
from other nests.

Q1 Under which subtitle is this information found?

The biggest ants are queen ants. _____

Tunnels lead into the ants' nest. _____

The big male ants die after they have mated with the queen. _____

Worker ants don't have wings. _____

Worker ants have many roles in the running of the nest. _____

Answer each of the questions with a sentence.

Q2 Two types of ants have wings. Which ants are they?

_____

Q3 How many eggs does the queen lay? _____

Q4 Which ants dig the tunnels? _____

Q5 Is there one ant that has the most important job? _____

Q6 Explain your answer to **Q5**.

_____

Q7 Write a fact about each type of ant.

Queen ant _____

Male ant _____

Worker ant _____

SCENE 1

(A busy train station crowded with travellers. Sasha and Omar arrive pushing an old fashioned pram and carrying a bag stuffed with belongings.)

Sasha   Don't say anything, Omar, let me do the talking.

Omar   *(into the pram)* You've got to keep quiet, Valentine, we're in the station now.

(They approach a soldier checking documents at the entrance to the platform.)

Soldier   Papers?

Sasha   *(handing over papers)* We're going to meet our mother. She's waiting for us.

Soldier   The baby – his pass?

Sasha   He's… a new baby, he doesn't have one.

Soldier   No papers, I can't let you through.

(Fran arrives with a huge suitcase and pushes in.)

Fran   Please – let an old woman by! My bad hip! My feet!

Soldier   *(unmoved)* Papers?

(Fran gives him her papers as the children watch.)

Soldier   Go through.

(Fran hurries through the barrier. Sasha grabs Omar and drags him after Fran, getting away from the soldier.)

Soldier   Hey you! Come back!

(Sasha and Omar disappear into the crowd.)

SCENE 2

(Fran staggers into the train compartment with her bundles.)

Sasha   Please, madam, if we could stay with you, we're on our own…

Fran   Oh no – impossible, I must have my space.

Sasha   The soldiers don't stop old people so much when they have children.

Fran   I don't like babies.

Omar   It isn't a baby – it's a dog.

(Sasha looks at him furiously.)

Lin Coghlan

Fill the missing gaps.

Q1 Sasha and Omar pushed a _____ into the train station.

Q2 _____ wanted to talk to the soldier.

Q3 The soldier wanted to look at Sasha and Omar's _____.

Q4 _____ pushes in while Sasha was talking to the soldier.

Q5 Fran doesn't like _____.

Answer each of the questions with a sentence.

Q6 Who are the children going to meet?

_____

Q7 Why does Omar tell Valentine to keep quiet?

_____

Q8 Why does Sasha want to stay with Fran?

_____

Q9 Why doesn't Fran want the children to stay with her?

_____

Q10 Copy a line from the play that illustrates each of these statements.

Fran is elderly. _____

Fran has walking problems. _____

Fran is rather grumpy. _____

Fran likes to be alone. _____

Transport

There are many different ways to travel and to move goods around. Sometimes people walk and use animals pulling carts to transport heavy items. Aircraft, ships, trains, cars and buses carry people and freight from one place to another. The way people and things are moved depends on how quickly they need to travel, and where they are going.

A container ship can carry much more than an aeroplane, but is much slower.

Trains can carry far more than trucks, but trucks are still needed to collect the goods from the train at the end of its journey.

Buses and coaches carry more people than cars, but don't usually take everyone to their final destinations, so some people prefer to travel by car if they have one.

Use words from the box to finish each sentence.

| car | carts | ship | trucks | bus |

Q1 Animals pulling _____ can transport heavy items.

Q2 A _____ can carry more goods or people than an aeroplane.

Q3 _____ collect goods at the end of a train journey.

Q4 A _____ or coach can carry more people than a _____.

Q5 Complete this table with the reasons for and against using different types of transport.

Transport type	Reason **for** using	Reason **against** using
bus		
ship		
car		
train		
lorry / truck		

Answer each of the questions with a sentence.

Q6 In the olden days many items were transported by barge on canals. Why do you think this no longer happens?

_____

Q7 Aeroplanes can quickly move freight around. Why aren't they used for everything?

_____

Q8 You want to send a small package to Australia. List the modes of transport it might need to reach its destination.

_____

The Wind in the Willows

Suddenly Mole, who was taking a rest on the river bank, noticed something…

As he sat on the grass and looked across the river, a dark hole in the bank opposite, just above the water's edge, caught his eye. Something bright and small seemed to twinkle down in the heart of it, vanish, then twinkle once more like a tiny star. But it could hardly be a star in such an unlikely situation, and it was too glittering and small for a glow-worm. Then, as he looked, it winked at him, and so declared itself to be an eye, and a small face began gradually to grow up round it, like a frame round a picture. A brown little face, with whiskers. A grave round face, with the same twinkle in its eye that had first attracted his notice.
Small neat ears and thick silky hair.
It was the Water Rat!

The Rat said nothing, but stooped and unfastened a rope and hauled on it, then lightly stepped into a little boat which the Mole had not observed. It was painted blue outside and white within, and was just the size for two animals, and the Mole's whole heart went out to it at once, even though he did not yet fully understand its uses.

The Rat sculled smartly across and made fast. Then he held up his fore-paw as the Mole stepped gingerly down. "Lean on that!" he said. "Now then, step lively!" and the Mole to his surprise and rapture found himself actually seated in the stern of a real boat.
"This has been a wonderful day!" said he, as the Rat shoved off and took to the sculls again. "Do you know, I've never been in a boat before in all my life."

Kenneth Grahame

Who did what? Answer 'Rat' or 'Mole'.

Q1 Who was having a rest? _____

Q2 Who peered out of a hole? _____

Q3 Who got in the boat first? _____

Q4 Who rowed the boat? _____

Q5 Who had never been in a boat before? _____

Answer each of the questions with a sentence.

Q6 What did Mole first notice on the opposite river bank?

_____

Q7 Using the picture and information from the passage, describe what Rat looks like.

_____

Q8 How big was Rat's boat?

_____

Q9 How did Mole feel when he was in the boat?

_____

Q10 What does each of these lines from the passage mean?

'A grave round face…' (line 8)	
'…which Mole had not observed.' (line 13)	
'Now then, step lively!' (line 17)	

Thrills City Adventure Park

Scariest rides ever!

Techno Ride

Vortex

The Brazen Beast

Mighty Meteor

Raging River's Revenge

An awesome day for all the family

Open 10 a.m. – 6 p.m. everyday
Close to motorway   Free parking

★ Escape on a once-in-a-lifetime adventure
★ Unlimited fun all year round
★ Live entertainment and characters
★ Surprises at every turn
★ Splash yourself silly in the water park!

★ Relax in our spa and health club
★ New this year – embark on an underwater adventure in the new sea life aquarium
★ Stay overnight at our special 4★ family-friendly hotel
★ Over the Rainbow Club – fab fun for our younger guests

★ Find us on Facebook and Twitter for all the latest news, chat and offers
★ 2 for 1 tickets before 13th July
★ Family Weekend Autumn Saver – save a huge 30%
★ Jump the queues and save 5% – print your tickets at home

Sign up now to receive the latest information and offers and become a Select Guest

Sign up

Title

Surname

Email

Answer these questions with a number.

Q1 What time does Thrills City shut? 6 p.m.

Q2 What percentage of the ticket price can you save if you print your ticket at home? 5 %

Q3 How many stars does the family-friendly hotel have? 4 ★

Q4 How much does it cost to park at the Adventure Park? £ 0

Q5 Before what date in July do you get 2 for 1 tickets? 13 th

---

Answer each of the questions with a sentence.

Q6 Why do you think the leaflet advertises that Thrills City is close to a motorway?

easy to see and get to

Q7 What activities at Thrills City are linked to water?

the water park and the raging rivers revenge

Q8 Why do you think adults will enjoy Thrills City too?

spa and health club live entertainment scairy rides

Q9 Where can you go to get more information about Thrills City?

on facebook and twitter

Q10 Imagine you are going to visit Thrills City. Write about why you want to go there and what you might do once you arrive.

I love riding roallicosters when I arrive I will go on evry ride ever !

A small dragon

I've found a small dragon in the woodshed.
Think it must have come from deep inside a forest
because it's damp and green and leaves
are still reflecting in its eyes.

I fed it on many things, tried grass,
the roots of stars, hazel-nut and dandelion,
but it stared up at me as if to say, I need
foods you can't provide.

It made a nest among the coal,
not unlike a bird's but larger,
it is out of place here
and is quite silent.

If you believed in it I would come
hurrying to your house to let you share my wonder,
but I want instead to see
if you yourself will pass this way.

Brian Patten

Use the words in the box to answer the questions.

grass   woodshed   hazel-nut   nest   leaves

Q1 Where was the dragon found? woodshed

Q2 What was reflected in his eyes? leaves

Q3 What was the dragon fed? hazelnut   ~~Att F~~grass

Q4 What did the dragon make amongst the coal? nest

Answer each of the questions with a sentence.

Q5 Where is it thought the dragon came from?

Deep inside the forest

Q6 Did the dragon like what it was fed?

No

Q7 Which line in the poem describes the size of the dragon's nest?

larger then a bird nest.

Q8 Do you think the dragon is real or has the poet imagined it?

hmm... ~~orcorse~~ of course its real (not).

Q9 The poem doesn't describe the dragon.
Write your own description of what this dragon looks like.

Red whith sharp teeth whith blood
on them as big as a lorry
and NOT I REPEAT NOT TO BE FEAD!

Answers

Go!
Page 4–5
1. Golly
2. west
3. Rose
4. horse
5. Betsy Byars
6. The sisters wanted to go west to perform songs and dances.
7. The sisters didn't find anything wrong with the horse.
8. The horse didn't understand the command 'Go'.
9. The sisters said 'Giddy-up!' to make the horse move.
10. e.g. Before: frustrated, cross, unhappy, grumpy, confused. After: happy, relieved, pleased, glad, overjoyed

I love our orange tent
Page 6–7
1. ✔
2. ✔
3. ✗
4. ✗
5. ✔
6. ✗
7. 'I love our orange tent' is repeated in the poem.
8. By repeating the line the poet is reinforcing how she feels about the orange tent.
9. The fifth verse states that the poet feels warm and safe inside the tent.
10. Child's own answer stating whether the description of the tent would be the same if it was a blue tent.
11. Child's own answer describing what they would see, hear and feel on a camping trip if there was thunder and lightning during the night.

Thunder and Lightning
Page 8–9
1. grumpy old sheep
2. Lightning
3. damage and noise
4. sky
5. Thunder
6. Nigerian
7. e.g.

Villagers' feelings at first	Villagers' feelings after a while
delighted relieved happy relaxed	frustrated tired unhappy grumpy

8. The village chief decided to banish Thunder and Lightning as they were disturbing the village with all their noise and damage.
9. Child's own answer describing how they think Thunder and Lightning will have felt once banished.

Motorway madness
Page 10–11
1. 1. A lorry carrying monkeys broke down.
   2. The lorry driver went to get help.
   3. A monkey lifted the latch on the lorry door.
   4. A monkey sat on top of a police car.
   5. The monkeys safely arrived at the zoo.
2. Child's own answer stating how they think the lorry driver felt, e.g. annoyed, foolish.
3. Child's own answer stating how they think Inspector Baker felt, e.g. amused, happy.
4. Child's own recount, imagining they were in a car watching the monkeys.

The lion and the mouse
Page 12–13
1. The mouse woke the lion by running over his paws.
2. The lion let the mouse go because the mouse persuaded him to, saying he might be able to help him one day.
3. The lion became caught in a hunter's net.
4. The lion escaped because the mouse bit through the ropes of the net.
5. small – little, flatten – crush, wandering – roaming, nibble – gnaw, large – huge
6. Child's own answer, e.g. don't suggest little things are of less use or value just because they are small.

From a railway carriage
Page 14–15
1. moving railway carriage
2. bridges and houses
3. tramp
4. a man and load
5. cattle – battle, plain – rain, brambles – scrambles
6. The poem mentions a cart and horse, a form of transport not often seen these days.
7. The poet is describing the fast speed the carriage travels at by using the line – 'Each a glimpse and gone for ever!'.
8. Four of the child's own sentences, describing things they passed during a trip in a car.

Oceans alive
Page 16–17
1. Oceans Alive
2. Angie Belcher
3. Collins
4. 44
5. Oceans under threat
6. 8
7. 38
8. 46
9. 9
10. 44
11. 10
12. Child's own answer, detailing a chapter they would add to the book, and a title for the chapter.
13. Child's own blurb written for this book, briefly describing what the book is about.